A VERY COCO CHRISTMAS

A SPARKLING, FEEL-GOOD, CHRISTMAS SHORT STORY

ROBERT BRYNDZA

RAVEN
STREET

Raven Street Publishing
www.ravenstreetpublishing.com
© Raven Street Limited 2021

eBook ISBN: 978-1-914547-03-4
Print ISBN: 978-1-8384878-3-6
ALSO AVAILABLE AS AN AUDIOBOOK

For Ricky and Lola, I know you can't read this, because you're dogs, but you make our lives complete.

DECEMBER 1985

SATURDAY 21ST DECEMBER

I never thought I would grow to love Aberystwyth so quickly. I thought I was a London girl through and through, but the dark beauty of Wales by the sea has captivated my heart. So too has Daniel Pinchard.

We woke up entwined this morning in my high little attic room, with its rather precipitous view of the paved seafront promenade below. A storm had raged all night, the waves smashing into the concrete wall of the prom throwing up giant jets of seawater that slapped against my window. The Christmas lights strung on wires along the street lamps swung and clinked and as the green, red and blue shone through the rippling water coursing down my window, they gave it a deliciously romantic feel. All through this my dark and gorgeous Daniel was naked in my bed. He sleeps naked, which is something quite thrilling. He has a lithe muscular body with a smattering of hair on his beautiful chest and stomach, and he has long chestnut hair, almost to his shoulders. His eyes are a warm caramel colour, his lips full, his nose strong and he always has a dark line of stubble on his square jaw. I'm hopelessly in love.

When I was preparing to come away to University my mother took me to buy 'a suitable nightie'. This wasn't because she wanted me to look good in bed for future lovers.

'You'll be sharing a house with other girls, and it's *Wales*.' She shuddered, thumbing through the racks of button-up-to-the-neck long nightgowns. 'You need to show you're cosmopolitan, but not easy... Now do you want flame proof?'

'In case some amorous suitor attacks me with a blow torch?'

'Don't be so ridiculous...' she snapped, marching off to the till with something long and frilly.

As I lay in only my knickers and no bra, watching Daniel sleep, I laughed at what my mother would think. The sea was now calm and there was just the caw of seagulls picking over the spoils thrown up by the storm and the drag of the waves on the shingle. I sat up and lit a cigarette. Daniel opened his eyes.

'Morning Coco,' he said stretching out his long, agile body.

'It's so romantic, after a storm,' I said, as the sun began to shine through the window. 'Look at the sea reaching out to the horizon glittering and smooth... infinite.'

'You have the most excellent tits,' said Daniel sitting up and taking a drag of my cigarette.

'Daniel!' I said. 'I was being romantic.'

'So was I,' he grinned. 'We've got three hours until we have to get the train back to London, let's make the most of it...' He leant over with a twinkle in his eye and stubbed out my cigarette, then pulled me on top of him.

An hour later we had dragged ourselves out of bed and I was packing my suitcase.

'Are the Bananas still here?' asked Daniel pulling on his

drainpipe jeans. I opened my door onto the landing and there was silence. The Bananas are my housemates Tania, Tanya and Claire. They'd already caught trains home for Christmas. The smell of them lingered though, a stench of hairspray, catching in the back of my throat with a sting. They're all Bananarama mad, and have their hair done accordingly which involves discharging a whole can of Aquanet Super Hold on their wet hair whilst blow-drying furiously. I've asked Daniel if I should try mine this way, but he says he loves my blonde hair long and natural.

Anyway, which Banana would you be?' he asked. 'Tania is Keren, Tanya is Sara and Claire is Siobhan. There's nothing worse than being second banana, let alone fourth.'

He had a point.

We left my flat with a suitcase each and Daniel had his battered guitar case slung over his shoulder. We walked hand in hand along the prom, and made a beeline for our favourite café, *Dai's*, a small squat building sandwiched between the amusement arcade and video shop on the pier. It used to be a serious rock-and-heavy-metal bar, until Dai bought it, a thin and wan Welshman with huge milky blue eyes. During term time it's home to most of the arts faculty and Dai plays pop music. We grabbed a seat by the window looking out to sea. The café was full of people chattering and smoking above the hiss of the coffee machine.

'Hello loves,' said Dai listlessly wandering over with his pad. 'I thought you'd be back in the smoke by now?'

'No, our train is at two-thirty,' I said sadly.

'Yes, Christmas again,' said Dai mournfully in his soft

Welsh lilt. 'It'll just be me and mother, if I don't strangle the old bag during *The Two Ronnies*... so, what will it be for the lovebirds?'

I looked at Daniel.

'I'm going to treat us. We'll have two of your big breakfasts please,' I said.

'Tea or coffee?'

'Tea.'

He wrote it down and took our menus,

'Won't be a mo, loves,' he said then wandered off to the kitchen.

'Coco,' said Daniel frowning. 'I was just going to have a cuppa.'

'You need the energy after last night,' I said trying to keep my voice light.

'You always treat me,' he said lowering his voice.

'Because I love you,' I said, my heart sinking that the subject of money had arisen, again. I pulled out my pack of cigarettes and offered him one, but he shook his head and began rolling his own with the minuscule amount of tobacco he had left.

We sat in silence looking out at the sea, Daniel sucking determinedly at his darning needle sized roll-up as it kept going out. Our breakfasts came soon after and he gobbled his down as the radio played *Merry Christmas Everyone*.

'Slow down, we've got time,' I said. Then I noticed him eyeing his guitar propped by the table.

'I'm gonna go and busk for an hour or so, then I'm going to pay for both our breakfasts,' said Daniel leaping up enthusiastically as soon as he'd finished his last mouthful.

'Don't... it's freezing, and...'

'And what? Not worth it for the few pence I get!'

'You get more than that,' I said but he'd grabbed his guitar and stalked out.

'He's a heartbreaker, that one,' said Dai wistfully, appearing at the table and staring at Daniel's angry wake. 'The bad boys always break your heart... Another cuppa love?'

'Go on then,' I said. I sat and smoked a cigarette with a fresh cup of tea, looking out at the sea and the gorgeous Edwardian houses lining the promenade. I would kill to just stay here with Daniel for Christmas, walking on the beach, lying in bed, whiling away hours with a cuppa and a fag in Dai's cosy little cafe. Daniel returned an hour later, thrilled.

'Look Coco!' he said. He tipped out the contents of his busking hat onto the table.

'You made *sixteen pounds*!' I said counting it out.

'I barely make a quid usually. Look, someone even gave me a fiver! A fiver for my playing! I can't believe it.' he said grinning broadly.

'I can.' I said. 'You're a brilliant musician.'

When Daniel went to pay at the counter, however, Dai was having none of it.

'It's on the house loves,' he said. 'Merry Christmas!'

'But I wanted to pay...' said Daniel.

'Treat 'er to somewhere nicer than this.' said Dai.

'No, I want to...'

'Hush those sweet lips,' grinned Dai putting his hand over Daniel's indignant mouth. 'Now bugger off home for Christmas.'

'Thanks, Dai, merry Christmas,' I said giving him a huge hug.

'Yeah, thanks, merry Christmas,' said Daniel begrudgingly. We suddenly realised our train was about to leave so grabbed our luggage and ran for it. I looked back at the sea front as we rounded the corner to the station. Then the sun went in and we were on the train and moving off towards London.

The journey was long and crowded. Daniel got into a row with the old man running the buffet car when he went to order us two cups of coffee (which were a rip-off at 49p each). He proudly went to pay with the five-pound note he'd earned, but the stupid old git refused to take it!

'Ow do I know thas' yours?' he asked, squinting at it as if it was a block of gold stolen from Fort Knox.

'Why wouldn't it be mine?' said Daniel. The old man looked at him sceptically in his tatty brown leather jacket. 'This is the fashion,' said Daniel, hurt.

'No, *thas'* the fashion,' said the old man, pointing at a boy standing behind us dressed in expensive Adam Ant gear.

I quickly rummaged in my handbag for some change, but Daniel told the old man and the Adam Ant boy to sod it and stormed off. I glared at the old man and followed Daniel. He'd had to eke out his tiny grant throughout the term, and now, the one time he was flush, that stupid old fool embarrassed him. He locked himself in the train toilet. (Daniel, not the Old Man) and when I finally persuaded him to come out around Swindon, his eyes were red from crying.

'You can buy me a coffee in London,' I said but it only made things worse.

It was dark when the train pulled into Euston. The station was dirty and smelly and everything seemed to be bathed in a dim fluorescent yellow. We fought our way through the crowds hand in hand and down to the northern line at Kings Cross. Then we had to say goodbye. We stood on the platform, trying to hear each other through the crowds of people surging past and the wind roaring along the tunnel.

'I love you Coco,' he shouted, wiping a tear from my cheek. 'Don't forget that, and it's only two weeks.'

'I'm going to miss you so much, I already miss you and you're here...' I shouted as his train clattered and roared up beside us.

'We're going to meet up and I'm going to take you to the cinema and for pie and mash... and let's phone each other every day,' he shouted leaning closer.

He pulled out a strip of photos we'd had taken at an instant photo booth in Boots a few days ago. He carefully tore the four pictures across the middle so that we had two each, and wrote his phone number on the back of his. I did the same and we swapped. Then his train was about to leave. He kissed me and jumped inside just as the doors closed. He looked at me through the door as the train slowly moved off. I stayed and watched until the back of it had vanished into the darkness of the tunnel, then I took the stairs up to the circle line and found a train to Baker Street.

It was so embarrassing to cry on the tube. It wasn't very busy. Sitting across from me was a girl with black lipstick and bright red hair in a huge spike three feet high. I thought she must use more hairspray than Tania, Tanya and Claire combined. She was sitting with a boy who was dressed like Boy George – he was even wearing eye shadow! They both had Christmas baubles on their ears and tinsel strung around their necks.

'You alright?' said the girl. She smiled and her black lipstick stretched and cracked showing pale lips underneath. She leaned across pressing a green paper towel into my hand that she must have got from a public toilet.

'Thanks.' I said dabbing my eyes politely with it.

'You got any fags?' demanded the boy sharply.

'Oh, um, yes...' I said. He stared at me, white eyes surrounded by black smudged eyeliner. I opened my handbag, pulled out my packet of cigarettes and offered him one.

'What about me?' said the girl, her voice hardening. 'I was just nice to you. I gave you a hanky...'

I felt like telling her that free bog paper was *not* a hanky but they'd both turned menacing.

'She's got a *load* of pound notes in her handbag too,' said the boy. Looking round I could see the train was pretty empty. My end of the carriage was sparse. A group of bored-looking commuters were sitting up the other end, engrossed in their broadsheets. I started to feel panicky.

'She thinks she's better than us, don't you think Mike?' said the girl licking the corner of her black-lipsticked mouth. Her tongue was fat and ripe and covered in white fur.

'Yeah. She *could* afford to give us the rest of her fags, she could just buy more...' said Mike.

Suddenly the train pulled into a station. I grabbed my suitcase, got up and ran off the train. I found myself on the platform under the fluorescent lights and kept running until I reached the stairs. I glanced back and saw that the train was now moving away and the platform was empty. I stopped, panting, and with a jolt of horror realised I'd left my handbag on the seat of the train. It had my cigarettes, ten pounds, and the photos of me and Daniel, *with his phone number written on the back*. In tears, I waited for the next train as it got colder and a thin fog began to fill the air.

When I arrived at Baker Street Station it was busy and warm. Christmas lights hung above the escalator and people were flooding past me in the opposite direction laughing and laden down with Christmas shopping. Office workers wore tinsel in their hair and at the top of the stairs a long-haired busker was playing an upbeat punk version of *God Rest Ye Merry Gentlemen* on his guitar. He made me think of Daniel.

Dad was waiting for me in his hat and coat by a cobbler's booth with droopy Christmas decorations hanging off the sign.

'Hello darling,' he said. 'I've missed you.' He gave me a big hug and I pressed my face against the scratchy material of his winter coat, still a little cold from outside. I suddenly felt like a child again and embarrassed. Could he tell I was no longer a virgin? Only a few hours ago my head had been lying against Daniel's naked chest... I blushed.

'Where's Mum?' I asked, changing the subject.

'She's getting ready for Christmas. We've got Yvonne and Adrian Rosebury coming over with Kenneth on Christmas Day.' I rolled my eyes. 'Now come on Karen,' he said.

It was so strange to be called Karen again. It felt like I had been Coco forever...I realised Dad was still rabbiting on.

'I'm sure they're keen to hear all about your time at university... and Kenneth is studying French at Keele so you'll have lots to talk about.'

'Will I? I'm studying English at the other end of the country.'

Dad let that slide as we continued walking, past the Clarence Gate entrance to Regent's Park. I could see the edge of the lake where it was frozen and a man in a threadbare suit was shivering next to a vat of roasting chestnuts.

I opened my mouth to say that I wanted to buy some chestnuts, but then remembered I'd lost my handbag.

I felt suffocated as we came through the front door. The central heating was on full blast, there was a strong smell of furniture polish and everything had a dull gleam to it. Mum was standing by the hall table, with the phone to her ear and adjusting her jet-black curls in the mirror. She looked ready to go into battle with Christmas, in an expensive red nylon blouse with huge shoulder pads, a tight black pencil skirt, and perilously high black stilettos. She mouthed dramatically that she *was on the phone,* and switched the receiver to the other ear so I could lean in for a hug.

Dad brought my case in behind him and she jabbed her finger at our feet and mouthed *SHOES.*

'What about her shoes?' I muttered but Dad grinned at me so we complied.

'Yes Yvonne, do bring your electric carving knife... we're so looking forward to seeing you and Adrian, and Karen hasn't stopped talking about how excited she is to see Kenneth.'

'When did I say that?' I muttered to Dad. Mum shot me daggers and lurched down the hall with the phone, the long wire following obediently into the living room as she pulled the door shut behind her.

'What a nice welcome,' I said.

'She means well, it's a lot to organise... Christmas. And it's the busiest time at the shop,' said Dad taking off his hat and hanging it up. 'You can still help out on Christmas Eve with all the Turkey orders?'

'Of course,' I said.

'We've missed you around here,' he said, kissing me on the forehead. Mum came out of the living room with the telephone and replaced it on the hall table.

'Yvonne and Adrian say hello, and Kenneth sent a special hello to you,' said Mum all twinkly-eyed. I pulled my face into a grin.

'How is he?' I said.

'Oh, he's doing wonderfully at Keele. Top of his class of course, and top of the athletics club.'

'Is he still as boring as hell?'

'You could do far worse than Kenneth Rosebury,' said Mum, giving me the once over. 'Oh Karen...' She patted me on the rump. 'What have you been eating? Your grandmother's big bottom seems to have skipped a generation.'

I shot an indignant look at Dad, but Mum carried on breezily saying,

'We've had the whole house redecorated. It's all Laura Ashley.'

The decor was far too much, the floral patterns looming until they seemed to crush me. I took my coat off and hung it beside Dad's and we went through to the living room. It looked beautiful with a huge Christmas tree by the bay window, decorated with tinsel and baubles. A fire was burning and hung above the fireplace were sprigs of holly and our three Christmas stockings.

'It's much nicer in here,' I said.

'Well we haven't done this room yet,' said Mum. She went to the record player, clicked on the turntable and placed the needle on a record. There was a crackle and the hushed warm harmony of *Silent Night* filled the room.

'Oh. Now isn't this elegant... Let's have a sherry, Bill,' she said. On cue Dad went to the sideboard and there was a soft chink as he pulled out three sherry glasses. 'I think you're grown up enough now for a little Emva Cream,' said Mum. I longed for a pint of lager with Daniel and suddenly had an image of him pressed against me whilst a storm raged outside my little attic room.

'Are you too warm darling?' asked Mum sitting on the sofa.

'I didn't realise you'd come back to us... so well insulated. I wouldn't have lit the fire.'

'No I'm fine,' I said gritting my teeth.

'So tell us all about Aberystwyth...'

I felt a screaming inside me. I wished I could tell them the truth, that I've got drunk and been skinny dipping in the freezing sea at night, that I know what a man looks like naked, and I've ignored Mum and *won't* be a virgin on my wedding night...

'What's *Wales* like?' she asked. 'We don't seem to get much time on the phone with you.' I bit my lip. I wanted to at least tell them about Daniel.

'I've made some good friends,' I said. 'Tania, Tanya and Claire...'

'Yes, and they're from London?' said Mum.

'Tania is from Highgate, Tanya from Chelsea and Claire is Scottish, from Fife.'

'Well... *two out of free aint bad*,' said Mum doing a terrible cockney accent then laughing at her own joke. 'Well, it's good they're local. I worried that you'd want lots of Welsh people over to stay,' she added in a relieved tone.

'What's wrong with Welsh people?' I said.

'Nothing, if they stay in Wales,' said Mum.

'Evelyn,' warned Dad.

'Well, I don't know why you decided to be so far away,' said Mum.

I bit my lip again, *shouldn't it be obvious, you silly cow? To get away from you!*

'Well, I'm glad you're having a lovely time,' said Mum. 'Now. We've lots to organise over the next couple of days. I missed you helping me with the tree.' She got up and crossed to the sideboard, pulling out a hand-painted glass bauble with *Karen* written across it in gold paint.

'I saved this for you, and the Fairy,' she said. I took it and went to the tree. As I reached up to hang it, the word Karen caught in the light.

'I need to discuss something with you both,' I said pulling the bauble away from the branch I'd chosen. They looked at me, confused, as if I'd deviated from the script that we've acted out every year since I was little.

'People at university... (*why couldn't I just say Daniel!*)... have given me a nickname,' I told them. 'They call me Coco and I like it, so I wondered if you'd call me Coco too.'

'What?' said Mum, ignoring her cardinal rule that you should always say pardon.

'At university,' I repeated carefully, 'people have given me the nickname Coco and I like it, a lot.'

This was crazy. I felt as though I was telling them I was a lesbian or something. Dad was looking to Mum for his next cue in this new script. Mum, who is rather good at improvisation when it involves being a bitch, responded.

'Coco? What a *horrible* nickname. No, no, no, I don't think so.'

'I'm an adult and it's important to me!' I could hear my voice rising in pitch and volume. I really wanted to tell them about Daniel but my courage was draining away.

'What? Important to you to sound like a *French prostitute!*' Mum stood up. I looked at Dad but he was making a move to go, draining the last of his glass.

'I'd better get to the shop and sort out some turkeys,' he muttered.

'Now look what you've done, Karen! You've *ruined* our Christmas tradition.'

'It's Coco!' I shouted. I was now furious, as much with myself as my mother. She stalked across the room, grabbed the fairy and impaled the poor thing on the top of the tree.

'There, happy now?' she snapped.

'What's your problem?' I said.

'You are. What's wrong with being Karen? It's a beautiful name. You know you're named after Karen Carpenter, although I wish you'd take a leaf out of her book and watch what you eat...'

'You're horrible!' I shouted.

'I'm only saying it because I care! You've come back a different person. I hope you're going to pull yourself together when the Rosebury's are here for Christmas lunch.'

'My name is now Coco,' I repeated.

'Oh no it's not,'

'I'm eighteen now, you can't stop me!' I shouted.

'But I can stop your allowance... and there won't be any more swanning around Wales like a French prostitute!' she shouted back.

'AAGH!' I shouted and stormed out slamming the living room door. I grabbed my suitcase and dragged it up the stairs two at a time and once in my room I slammed that door too.

SUNDAY 22ND DECEMBER

10.00 am My mother has sent me to Coventry. Well not literally, although I'd quite like to spend Christmas away from HER. No, I overheard her telling Dad after breakfast that she is *sending me to Coventry for a couple of days*. She won't be talking to me. How bloody Famous Five can you get? I swear they were the only books that ignorant woman ever read out loud with me at bedtime. Oh, and that Joan Collins book on how to turn yourself into Joan Collins.

I wish I hadn't left my handbag on that stupid train, then I'd have money and I could go somewhere. Coventry, maybe. And of course I'd have photos of Daniel to look at and his phone number. I swear I'm starting to forget what he looks like – and he hasn't phoned. Mum won't keep the phone book or the yellow pages in the hall because she thinks it looks common. Oh! The phone is ringing, it might be Daniel!

10.30 am It was Tania and Tanya from a phone box in Highgate. They just met up for coffee and are delighted because they've both been told they can have nose jobs from Father Christmas. I made a joke, asking how Father Christmas can fit a nose job down the chimney but the line was bad and they misunderstood and thought I was saying their noses were too huge to fit down the chimney. They hung up on me and then didn't pick up when I called back. So now my new friends hate me too.

12.00 pm Just back from an expedition to find a phone book. Four phone boxes on Marylebone High Street were devoid of phone books and stank of wee. Finally found one in Hanover Square, the park off Oxford Street. There are six Pinchard's in the phone book. Using some coppers I found in my moneybox I rang them all; none of them knew a Daniel Pinchard.

Now I'm paranoid Daniel gave me a false surname. I'm racking my brains to think if I've seen anything official with his name on it. I haven't.

12.15 pm I have! His jacket! His mother had sewn 'DANIEL PINCHARD' in the back of his jacket. Wonder what his mother is like? She can't be worse than mine.

4.30 pm Phone rang again. I hoped it was Daniel, Tania or Tanya, but it was Claire calling from Scotland. She also hates being back at home. Her parents sound even stricter than mine. Her father runs a kilt making business and with Hogmanay coming up she has to help out in their shop for the next fortnight. I told her that I have to get up at four in the morning and help out in Dad's butcher's shop on Christmas

Eve, but it didn't sound as bad. She wished me a happy Christmas and promised that she would talk to Tania and Tanya about the nose down the chimney mix up.

8.00 pm Am in bed surrounded by my childhood toys: dolls house, wooden horse, Sindy dolls etc. Why did my mother put them all back whilst I was away? Have had a horrible thought, what if I fall down the stairs and end up an invalid... I'll be stuck in this room for ever surrounded by my toys from childhood. No friends, no Daniel, just my mother bringing up soup on a tray... Her shoulder pads getting bigger and bigger until she has to negotiate doors sideways. I can't sleep. I wonder what Daniel is doing.

10.00 pm I just screamed so loudly that Dad came rushing in.

'What is it love?' he asked blearily. I told him I'd had a nightmare, and he went back to bed. I was too embarrassed to tell him that when I rolled over and lent on my glow-worm, its huge face lit up, scaring me half to death.

MONDAY 23RD DECEMBER

The doorbell rang early in the afternoon and I heard a familiar voice start to sing *Good Kind Wenceslas*. I came down the stairs two at a time and Daniel was standing in the open doorway his dark handsome face framed by his gorgeous long hair. He was singing beautifully, his voice carrying through the cold still air. I came to the bottom of the steps and joined Mum who was rapt with attention, actually clasping her pearls in joy. I'm sure if she'd known that this was the boy I had spent many a night lying underneath she wouldn't have been so joyful, but I just watched, grinning knowingly at him as he entertained my mother.

When he came to the end of the carol there was a brief silence as his voice faded, until we became aware of the sounds from outside once more, the cars rushing past at the end of the road, a bus hissing and roaring as it changed gear.

'Thank you, young man,' said Mum. 'What a lovely rendition of Good King Wenceslas.'

'Thanks,' said Daniel. 'I'm studying for a degree in music.'

'How impressive,' said Mum. 'I've always thought it's a very broad subject, classical, modern...'

'I'm studying classical, the history of music. Do you know how Good King Wenceslas liked his pizza?' said Daniel.

'No, I don't,' said Mum.

'Deep and crisp and even,' grinned Daniel. I burst out laughing but Mum looked blank.

'It was a joke, Mum,' I said cringing.

'Oh, yes... Look I don't usually do this, but come into the hall a moment out of the cold.' Daniel came in and wiped his feet on the mat. Mum closed the door behind him.

'Karen just stay here with...'

'Daniel.'

'Just stay here with Daniel whilst I find him something to be on his way with.'

She adjusted her cardigan and went off down the hall to the kitchen. The door swung closed behind her.

'What are you doing?' I said thrilled to see him.

'You didn't ring me Coco, and when I phoned you, your mum kept saying you weren't in.'

'Did she now,' I said, darkly. 'I thought you'd gone off me... I lost my handbag on the train with your number in and...'

It was odd and thrilling to see Daniel standing in the hallway of my house in London. His presence was sexy and dangerous against the pastel flocked wallpaper. He leant in and kissed me. His mouth was a mixture of hot and cold and he tasted of cigarettes and sweets. His stubble rubbed against my chin and I felt warmth flood through me. We jumped apart as the kitchen door opened and Mum came back. *This is ridiculous* I thought, and I stood up straight in preparation to tell her that Daniel was my boyfriend.

'Here we are, I've popped in some vegetables we've got spare.' She handed Daniel a package wrapped up in the pale pink of the *Financial Times* and tied with string. It was a food parcel. Everything about it screamed charity.

'Um... Thanks,' said Daniel trying to hide his embarrassment.

'I thought it was the least we could do, in the cold, well – it should keep you going.' Daniel looked like he wanted the floor to open up and swallow him. Mum leaned around him and opened the latch on the door.

'Do you have a phone number?' I said.

'Karen!' shrilled Mum.

'What? He's a musician, we might know people who need a carol singer...'

'I don't think so, Karen.'

Now the sound of his beautiful voice had faded, Mum saw she had an oik in a leather jacket perilously close to her Laura Ashley wallpaper.

'It's Catford 67932,' said Daniel quickly.

'Catford 67932,' I repeated.

'Merry Christmas,' he said and he walked off down the steps trying to regain his composure.

'Oh Karen,' said Mum closing the door. 'He's nice to look at but you could do so much better. Kenneth, for instance.'

'Why are you so obsessed with Kenneth? Do you fancy him?'

'If I were lucky enough to be young like you I'd be thrilled to have the pick of an eligible young man like Kenneth. And his father Adrian is a meat distributor and Yvonne tells me the Masonic Lodge are interested in him.'

I started to tell her about Daniel but the phone rang, and it was one of her reptilian Joan Collins friends who she talked to for nearly two hours. Which was long enough for me to lose my courage.

However, Daniel still loves me!

TUESDAY 24TH DECEMBER – CHRISTMAS EVE

We had to be up at three-thirty this morning to have the butcher's shop open to cope with the Christmas Eve rush. At four a queue had started to form outside in the dark.

I don't know why Dad asks Mum to help out, she just upsets everyone. She's always rude to Tom and Liam the two Saturday lads who come in to help, and she insists on wearing catering whites with full makeup and her best jewellery. Dad and I were both hoping there wouldn't be a repeat of last year when she lost her gold bracelet up a Turkey. Having to root around in four hundred turkeys' arses while she screamed the place down was not fun.

From the moment the shop opened we argued about everything. I wanted to play Capital FM for the Christmas music, but Mum wanted a tape of traditional Christmas carols, we bickered about who should take the money and who should wrap the turkeys, which escalated into raised voices about how the turkeys should be wrapped. At this point Dad came out in front of the long queue and said in a low voice.

'You two need to behave yourselves!'

'What do you mean *you two*?' said Mum shocked. 'She's a teenage girl, I'm...'

'You're just as bad,' he hissed. A truce was called for a few minutes until a lady came to the counter who looked in a real state. She had a kind face but her clothes were tatty and her hair unkempt. When she opened her purse to pay, she was five pence short.

'You need to come back when you can pay the full balance,' said Mum condescendingly. The woman's eyes filled with tears. I had some change in my pocket so I pulled a five pence piece out and dropped it in the till.

'Merry Christmas,' I said.

The woman smiled gratefully at me, and went off with her bag bulging with turkey. Mum snapped and grabbed me by the back of my catering jacket and dragged me past the queue of customers and into the walk-in freezer.

'Get off me!' I said in shock.

'Karen. Don't you dare do that again,' she said.

'It's five pence, the difference between someone eating and not eating on Christmas day!'

'What if we did that for everyone? We'd go bust! Your grandfather started this business with nothing, nothing! He worked his fingers to the bone so you can have all the things you take for granted. Your nice clothes, and silly records, and that handbag which cost a fortune which you lost on public transport!'

'Do you care about the poor?'

'Of course I do.'

'You're a liar. You thought that woman out there was dirt, and you thought that carol singer yesterday was too!'

'What?'

'Daniel. The carol singer... You gave him a load of old

vegetables when you should have given him money, he's hugely talented and funny and...'

'That's enough!' she snapped. 'Now pull yourself together and get out there and start behaving.'

'Like you?'

'Yes.'

'No. Never.' I said.

'What?'

'I quit.'

I took off my white coat and threw it at her. I stormed past my confused father who was lugging a huge ham, and out onto Marylebone High Street. The freezing wind was blowing diagonally, and sliced across my legs but I kept running. After a few minutes my run became a trudge and I found myself back at the phone box behind Oxford Street. I yanked open the door and went in out of the wind. I pulled some two pence pieces from my pocket, lifted the receiver and dialled the number Daniel had given me. After a few rings I heard the beeps and pushed the money in.

''Ello... Catford six, seven, nine, free, two...' my heart lurched. I hadn't thought Daniel's mother would answer. ''Oo's this?' said the voice.

'Oh, erm, hello. Um, I'm Karen, Coco, I'm a friend of Daniel's. Could I please speak to him?'

There was a muffled sound as she covered the phone.

''Ere Meryl love, there's some plummy girl on the blower for Danny...'

'He's gone up the shop for matches and tobacco...' said a younger reedier version of Daniel's mother. The sound unmuffled and she came back on the line.

'He's gawn up the shops for a packet h'of cigarettes,' she said suddenly sounding posh.

'How long ago did he leave?' I said.

'Abaht fifteen minutes h'ago.'

'And is the shop far?'

'Not v'hery, a mere hawp skip and h'ajump.'

'How long does it usually take him?' I said, now feeling desperate to talk to him.

''Oo d'ya think I am, Doris Stokes?' snapped the voice dropping all pretence of poshness. ''E'll be back when 'e's back!'

I said I was waiting in a phone box, gave her the number and asked if he could phone me as soon as he was back.

'Are you in the family way?' she said.

'What?'

'Ringing 'im from a phone box?'

'No, I...'

''Cos my Danny, 'e's a good boy. 'E got into university and what with 'is modules, an essays, 'e 'asn't got time to go round putting girls in the family way.'

I explained I was at university with Daniel and that I just wanted to wish him a happy Christmas. She reluctantly said she'd give him the number and put the phone down.

Snow had started to fall outside and the sky was getting dark. I tried not to feel gloomy. I was hungry and cold in a stinking phone box. A car pulled past and its headlights firing off the ice crystals on the window dazzled me. And then the phone rang! I picked up the receiver.

'Hello, is this the halfway house for girls in the family way?'

'Is that you, Daniel?'

'Of course it is, Coco. Why are you in a phone box?'

'I ran away from my mother.'

'Coco, how old are you?'

'I'm nearly nineteen.'

'Exactly. Which means that you are free to do what you want.'

'But you don't understand...'

'I think I do. You're a damsel in distress who needs rescuing?'

I laughed. 'Are you going to come and rescue me on a white steed?'

'Well close, I'll get my sister Meryl to drive me over to you in her new Ford Anglia.'

'To go where?'

'To come here.'

'You want me to come to your house?' I said.

'Of course,' he said. 'I want you to meet me mum.' I heard his mother in the background say, ''oo d'ya want me to meet? I've still got the turkey to pluck!' Daniel put his hand over the receiver.

'Mum you can pluck it later!' He came back on the line. 'Where are you?'

'Are you sure it's okay?' I could hear Daniel's mother still moaning in the background.

''Course it is, and my sister Meryl wants to get out for some fresh air and show off her new car.'

I gave Daniel the address of the phone box and replaced the receiver. Blimey. I was about to meet his family. He must be serious about me. Then I was filled with terror – what if they hate me?

Forty tense, freezing minutes later, I heard a low whining noise a bit like a plane coming in to crash-land. A pea-green Ford Anglia zoomed round the corner of Hanover Square with steam escaping from beneath the bonnet. A young woman with long brown hair was poking her head out of the driver's window trying to see past the steam. Daniel's head appeared out of the passenger window. I came out of the phone box and waved at them.

'Here she is, pull in here Meryl,' said Daniel. The car swerved and came to a stop beside the pavement. When the engine was off, the car let out an exhausted hiss and even more steam. Daniel opened the door and grabbed me in a big hug. I put my hand up and ran my fingers through his hair, which smelt divine. His sister Meryl got out of the driver's side and came round to the front. She was only in her twenties, a little older than Daniel, and dressed like a beatnik in a donkey jacket, brown chord trousers and a long green roll neck jumper.

'Fiddlesticks!' she exclaimed slamming her hand on the bonnet.

'She's stopped swearing since she joined the young conservatives,' said Daniel out of the corner of his mouth. I smiled at her and said hello. Meryl turned and gave me the once over.

'So this is Coco,' she said. She seemed surprised, like maybe she was expecting a stripper in nipple tassels and not the nice winter coat I was sporting. I suddenly wondered what kind of girls Daniel usually went out with. I got the impression he was more experienced, and he certainly hadn't needed a map the first time we...

'Hello,' I said snapping out of my head. 'Daniel's told me so much about you,' I said automatically.

'Has he? What?' said Meryl heaving up the car bonnet. I realised Daniel hadn't really told me anything about his older sister, other than that she was a bit weird and frigid.

'I hear you're a Tory?' I said hopefully.

'Which means you're not,' she said. 'I thought a nice girl

like you would shy away from Socialism - I can't imagine your family, being as well-to-do as they are, would contemplate going back to the eighty-three per cent tax rate and the frankly potty policies bandied about by that old fool Michael Foot!'

I stared at her. 'Um, I don't really follow politics,' I said. There was an awkward silence as she opened the bonnet and we all peered at the workings of the car engine.

'I think it needs some water,' said Meryl finally. 'Daniel, see if that pub will give you some.'

Daniel grinned and went off. We stood there in silence for a moment as the car began to make a ticking sound.

'What do you do, Meryl?' I said.

'I'm a typist at my local doctor's surgery,' she said, a little defensively.

'Oh. Do you find you get a lot of bugs?' I asked.

'No, I've been there for a few years now, and I've built up my immunity...' I wondered why she'd agreed to come all this way and pick me up. I wasn't getting much warmth from her.

Then I asked her about the car and she started to talk proudly about how she'd saved up for it. It had cost five hundred pounds, which was over two months' wages.

'Did it take you a long time to save all that?' I asked, pleased I'd hit on a good topic of conversation.

'Yes, although my housekeeping takes a dent out of wages; Mum doesn't get much from her job as a cleaner. How much do you pay your mother in housekeeping?' she asked.

'Um... I've never had to,' I said sheepishly.

'So you get to keep all your wages?'

'I'm a student... and my parents give me an allowance,' I blushed.

'Aren't you lucky,' said Meryl giving me an icy stare.

'I do work, when I'm home,' I added. 'My father owns a butcher's in Marylebone.'

'I've heard,' said Meryl. There was another silence, she pursed her lips and tapped her nails impatiently on the pea-green paintwork of the car's bonnet.

Oh God, I thought. *She hates me.* Luckily Daniel came running out of the pub with a huge glass lemonade bottle full of water and a funnel. He unscrewed the cap on the radiator and filled it up. Meryl looked on proudly as he leaned into the car and started the engine with a roar.

'Marvellous!' she said closing the bonnet with surprising force. A very pretty young blonde barmaid in a low-cut white shirt and too much makeup came out of the pub.

'Daniel... Have you finished with my funnel?' She grinned. 'The landlord needs it back.' Daniel went over to her.

'Could her skirt be any shorter?' I muttered as she put a hand on his arm and took back the bottle with the funnel. She pulled out a sprig of plastic mistletoe and held it above their heads. Daniel did that faux *if I must* shrug I've seen men do when they're confronted by a pretty girl, and leant in for a kiss – on the cheek admittedly – but rage boiled up inside me.

'Daniel, your sister is waiting and so am I!' I snapped, sounding horribly like my mother. Daniel came running back with lipstick on his cheek. Meryl looked at us both with a wry smile and we got into the car, me in the back. As we drove off, the barmaid was still standing at the edge of the kerb. Her pointy little breasts were poking through her tight little blouse. 'So, we're all good?' said Daniel.

'Who was she?' I said.

'I dunno, a barmaid,' he grinned.

'Well...' I huffed and stared out of the window. Meryl

glanced at me out of the corner of her eye and handed Daniel a tissue. He grabbed it and scrubbed at the lipstick.

'She was just being nice,' he said.

'It's fine,' I huffed trying to sound carefree. I was coming across badly. I wanted Meryl to like me.

London was very drab, everyone looked bored and pale struggling under the burden of shopping bags and the decorations seemed flaccid. The tinsel strung along Oxford Street was thin and drooping like the elastic that had gone on a large pair of pants.

'What are you saying about a large pair of pants?' asked Meryl. I'd been talking out loud.

'That's just Coco,' grinned Daniel grabbing my hand. 'She's very creative; she's going to be a writer.'

'Well I write, so I *am* a writer,' I said.

'Oh. What have you had published?' needled Meryl.

'Nothing yet,' I said blushing.

'I've read her stories, she's great,' said Daniel.

As we got closer to his house I realised how ridiculous I was. I'd run away from my mother as if I was ten years old. I should have just told my parents about Daniel, and then had him over for a cup of tea – or arranged to do something properly with him.

When we'd crossed the river south, I noticed how run-down the houses were becoming, brickwork blackened from hundreds of years of coal fires, and there were kids on swings, mothers in curlers with housecoats poking out under their winter coats. Meryl turned into a street with a broken sign and parked by an end-of-terrace house. It was almost dark and many of the houses had switched on their Christmas lights but still hadn't drawn the curtains.

We didn't walk up the front path to the door, but swung

round the side of the house and Daniel reached up and undid the latch on the back gate. We went through and down a long dank passage between the two rows of terraced houses. We came to another gate and Daniel reached up again for the latch. It opened onto a concrete yard that can't have been more than eight feet square. There was a coal house with a spade resting outside covered in a fresh layer of coal dust. A bit in the corner was fenced off with some twisted chicken wire, and inside was the most enormous turkey! His black and grey plumage was stunning and glinted as he scrabbled about in the dirt with a powerful red-clawed foot. Standing beside the pen was a woman, similar in height to Meryl. I'd say she was in her fifties. She had jet-black hair (obviously dyed) and swept back from her face in a little beehive. She had on those pointy glasses from the 1970s and a winter coat over a flowery housecoat.

'I din't expect you back so quick,' she said quickly closing her coat and putting her hand up to her mouth.

'Thas' alright, Mum,' said Daniel. 'This is Coco.' I held my hand out.

'It's lovely to meet you Mrs. Pinchard, you've got a beautiful home.' I don't know why I said that, I was so nervous.

''Ow do you know?' she asked suspiciously, her hand still in front of her mouth. ''Ave you 'ad 'er up in yer room? Danny, what 'ave I told you?'

'Mum! No,' said Daniel. 'No. Coco's just being nice,'

'Yes, what I meant is that... Um...' I cast my eye around to find something to compliment, but the squalid back yard made it hard. 'You've got a lovely turkey...'

'Yeah, 'e is lovely...' she said dropping the accusing tone. 'By rights 'e should be dead an' plucked but 'e's... clever, sensitive.'

I could see her point, turkey's usually have cruel little eyes, but this one had a soft mournful stare.

'I call 'im John-Paul,' said Mrs. Pinchard.

'After the Pope?' I asked, wondering if Daniel came from a strict Catholic family.

'No! Not 'im... John Paul Belmondo.'

'The French actor?'

'Ooh yeah, 'e's lovely. If I were a few years younger I'd bugger off to France for the chance to meet John Paul Belmondo.'

Meryl rolled her eyes. I put my hand out and John Paul the turkey let me lean in and touch his feathers, which were so soft. He sniffed at my hand and then looked up at us again with his mournful eyes.

'Meryl, Danny, I think we're jus' gonna 'ave chipolatas tomorrow,' said Mrs. Pinchard.

'I'm on a diet mum, I told you,' said Meryl moving past to the back door.

'As long as we get pud, I don't care,' said Daniel. 'Come on Coco, let's go inside.' Mrs. Pinchard got all flustered and told us to wait in the yard whilst she cleared up.

'It's really no problem,' I said, but she bustled off and Daniel followed her inside closing the door. I just caught her saying, 'You din't even give me a chance to put me bloody teeth in!'

I looked up at the row of terraces. Lights were going on and tantalising smells of baking wafted over the fences towards me. The snow began to fall more heavily and John Paul shifted on his huge feet and leaned into me from his side of the chicken wire. I know it's an odd thing to say about a turkey, but he really was sweet. I undid the latch on the makeshift little gate and I went into the pen. He let me gently brush the snow off his shiny black feathers, and he put his beak in my pocket then nibbled at one of my buttons. I thought guiltily of the rows of turkeys I'd seen earlier in the walk-in freezer.

'How could anyone eat you?' I said. He stopped nibbling and rested his head against my jacket blinking. I had never suspected this morning, that by the afternoon I'd be talking to a turkey in Daniel's back garden. I noticed there was a little wooden shelter in the corner of the pen and I fluffed up the pile of straw underneath it and John Paul walked over and made himself comfortable. Suddenly the back door opened and Daniel said I could come in. I gave the turkey another cuddle and followed him indoors.

The back door led into a small and beautifully clean kitchen decorated in orange and black patterned wallpaper. Blue Formica cupboards and work surfaces lined the walls and a matching blue Formica table filled the centre of the room. There was a warm smell of freshly-baked fruitcake mingled with gas from the stove that had just been lit. Daniel's mother was now wearing a smart blue dress and a cream cardigan, she also had her teeth in. She put a kettle on the gas and pulled out a tea caddy. Three Cadbury's advent calendars were propped up on the windowsill above the sink and there was tinsel strung around the glass lampshade, which hung above the kitchen table.

'Have a sit down,' said Daniel. 'Cup of tea?'

'Yes please,' I said pulling out a chair.

'Not that one,' snapped Mrs. Pinchard shoving the chair back in. I noticed a small tear in the plastic of the seat cushion. She pulled out the chair opposite.

'You get the view outside,' she said. I nodded and sat down, the snow was now swirling in eddies outside the window.

'You must be used to a much bigger place,' said Daniel helping me out of my coat and hanging it by the back door. I noticed his mother smoothing back her hair in the reflection of the boiler as she busied herself drying teaspoons with a tea towel.

'This is nice, cosy...' I enthused. I didn't know if that was a compliment or not, but I meant it. It was a lovely, warm and friendly place. Mrs. Pinchard carried on getting the tea ready. I had the feeling she didn't like me. Daniel went to the cupboard and started pulling down some mugs.

'Sit down Danny,' she ordered. 'She'll 'ave a cup an' saucer, like we usually 'ave!' She put the mugs back and left the room. Daniel reached across the table and grabbed my hand.

'I don't think your Mum likes me,' I whispered.

'No. You're getting the best crockery, this is good,' he grinned. 'We never use it,' he added with a whisper.

''Ere we are,' said Mrs. Pinchard coming back in with a tray of china cups, a milk jug and sugar bowl. 'I 'ad it out this morning for elevenses with friends.'

Daniel grinned at me and shook his head. I noticed a small fireplace under a mirror in the corner, wood and coal were built up neatly, with some newspaper and ready to be lit. Meryl came in and threw the post on the kitchen table. She grabbed a box of long matches and struck one. She lightly touched it to the newspaper and the fire burst to life, blazing within seconds.

'My Dad is hopeless at building fires,' I said breaking the silence. 'He's there for ages feeding it with wood and re-lighting it. That's a great fire. Did Mr. Pinchard build it?'

'You mean, Danny? Yes, 'e did,' said Mrs. Pinchard. The kettle began to whistle and she lifted it off the stove and poured a little hot water into the teapot.

'No, I meant Daniel's father, Mr. Pinchard.' I added. She swilled the hot water round the teapot, warming it up, and then tipped it into the sink with a practised move.

''Ow long 'ave you two been stepping out?' she said spooning tea leaves into the pot.

'Mum, I told you, me and Coco got together in September.'

'Well, it can't be that serious if yer didn't tell 'er yer dad's dead!'

'Oh. Oh, I'm sorry,' I said.

'I don't like to talk about it,' said Daniel squeezing my hand apologetically

''E died twelve year ago. Silly bugger went 'an got 'imself run over by a bus,' said Mrs. Pinchard. The kettle came back to the boil and began to scream. I didn't know what to say.

We sat as Mrs. Pinchard filled the teapot, then brought the cups over. She thumbed through the post and opened an envelope containing a Christmas card.

''Ere, speak of the devil, iss a card from Alf Watson, the bloke who dug yer dad's grave... 'e sends me a card every year.'

'How morbid,' said Meryl sitting beside me.

''E's got a son, Tony, works as 'is assistant. 'Ere, Meryl, why don't I give Alf a tinkle. Maybe you could go up the Odeon with Tony one afternoon?'

'I'm not going to the cinema with a gravedigger's assistant!' said Meryl indignantly.

'Why not?'

'For starters we have nothing in common,' said Meryl.

''Is dad dug your dad's grave!' said Mrs. Pinchard.

'I don't believe you Mum!' shouted Meryl.

'Well, yer not getting any younger my girl. You need to get yerself married orf. An' there's good money in death. You gonna work for that Doctor forever?'

Meryl got up in tears and stormed out slamming the kitchen door. Mrs. Pinchard seemed unperturbed and turned her attention to me.

'So, Coco,' she said pouring the tea. 'Yer at University with *my* Danny.'

'Yes, I am. I'm studying English Literature.'

'What yer gonna do with that when yer leave?' she asked, handing us cups and sitting down on the ripped chair.

'I'm going to be a writer.'

Mrs. Pinchard nodded.

'And what does yer dad do? If e's alive that is?'

'Her father owns a butcher's,' said Daniel. Mrs. Pinchard suddenly looked interested.

'Oh, well thas very nice. A butcher, I'd like a butcher in the family.' Then she actually smiled at me. 'Iss lovely to meet yer Coco.'

This was good! She suddenly seemed to have warmed to me. The happy moment was interrupted by a knock at the back door and a voice said,

'Cooo-eee!' An older lady in a housecoat and hairnet poked her head round the door.

'Who's that?' I said quietly to Daniel.

'Mrs. Roberts, the next door neighbour.'

'Ooh sorry Ethel, I didn't realise you 'ad company...' said Mrs. Roberts.

'Don't worry love, come in. 'Ere, this is Danny's nice new girlfriend, Coco. 'Er dad's a butcher!'

'Nice to meet you love,' said Mrs. Roberts.

Mrs. Pinchard called me his girlfriend. She approved!

'I won't keep ya, Ethel,' said Mrs. Roberts. 'I just wanted to see John Paul Belmondo all trussed up for the oven. I don't know 'ow yer did it...'

'What love?' said Mrs. Pinchard cutting the fruitcake.

'I don't know how you slaughtered that sweet little turkey.'

'No I can't bring meself to do it...' said Mrs. Pinchard.

'Oh, I thought 'cos 'e's gawn?'

'What d'yer mean, gawn?'

'John Paul, the turkey 'e's gawn! 'E's not in the yard. Both gates are open!' said Mrs. Roberts. It suddenly dawned on me. I'd left the gate open.

'Oh no... I think it was me,' I said.

'What?' said Mrs. Pinchard.

'I left the gate open!'

'What the bloody 'ell did yer do that for!' shouted Mrs. Pinchard. Everyone leapt up and we jostled outside. A thick layer of snow now covered the yard. The moon had come out and it was so bright. The gates were indeed open. John Paul Belmondo was nowhere to be seen.

'That was me Christmas Turkey!' shrilled Mrs. Pinchard. 'Six months of saving in the Christmas club!'

'I'm so sorry,' I said. 'It was an accident.'

'And I left the other gate open,' said Daniel helpfully.

'Well yer both bloody fools!' she shouted.

We split up and searched the length of the road out front, and the neighbours' gardens calling out, *'Jean Paul Belmondo,'* like a bunch of depressed fans of French new wave cinema. But no turkey came trotting up. I felt terrible, not only had I lost them their Christmas lunch but Mrs. Pinchard was mourning the loss of a beloved pet. When we re-grouped in the back garden I saw it was almost seven o'clock.

'Daniel,' I said awkwardly. 'I've just realised I should get home... I don't know what to do about this?'

Mrs. Pinchard was still ranting to Mrs. Roberts saying, 'The poor bugger is long gone, knowing this lot round 'ere. 'E'll be in someone's oven, I've no doubt.'

Daniel went over to his mum and she broke down in tears with her head on his shoulder.

'Oh Danny, why did yer 'ave to bring...'

'What?'

'No, It's not 'er fault, I'm sure she's a nice girl...' she burst into tears again.

'Do you think your dad has a spare turkey?' said Daniel over his mother's shoulder.

'We've got nothing to eat tomorrow,' sobbed Mrs. Pinchard. 'Only five chipolatas and box of Quality Street...'

I thought of the pantry at home, filled to bursting with meat and fresh food. I then pictured our dining room: lots of space and a huge table.

'Come to my house for lunch tomorrow,' I blurted. 'The three of you,' I added, as Mrs. Roberts from next door seemed to think she might get an invite too.

'We'd love to,' said Mrs. Pinchard suddenly regaining her composure. 'What time does yer dad carve?'

Daniel looked shocked. 'Hang on Coco, are you sure. Your house, in Marylebone?'

'Course she's sure!' said Mrs. Pinchard.

'Yes. Course,' I said, but inside I was panicked at what I'd just offered.

'Shall I give yer mum a tinkle?' Said Mrs. Pinchard. 'See if she wants them chipolatas?'

'No, it's fine. Look we eat at one, so why don't you come for midday?' I said the colour draining from my face. All Mrs. Pinchard's tears for John Paul Belmondo had vanished, and she hurried inside.

'Meryl!' she yelled, 'make yerself useful and plug in the Carmen rollers! We're goin' up west for Christmas lunch!'

I was left with Daniel in the moonlight.

'Are you sure you want to do this?' he asked. He pushed my hair away and leant in and kissed my neck.

'Yes. I love you,' I said. 'And I want your mum to like me too.'

'You are the most amazing woman. I love you,' he said. His brown eyes glinted in the moonlight and I wanted him so bad. He kissed me softly.

'Why don't you stay here?' he asked, smiling.

'What? Tonight? In your room?'

'No. I don't think my mother would approve of that... even if you have invited her over for Christmas lunch. No, you can have my bed, I'll have the settee and then when everyone is asleep, I'll stealthily climb the stairs...'

'Avoiding the creaky ones...'

'Yes avoiding the creaky ones,' he grinned, 'and I'll ravish you in my bed...' I could feel him getting stiff. I looked around but there was no one to see us.

'Jeez the thought of doing you under my poster of The Smiths,' he growled.

'You like The Smiths?'

'Okay - the Electric Light Orchestra,' he admitted. I laughed.

'No I should go home,' I said. 'I need to sort things out for tomorrow... tell my mother.'

'Well you won't get a train or a bus on Christmas Eve. I'll drive you.'

'Can you drive?'

'I haven't passed my test, but yeah. And who's going to check on Christmas Eve?'

Daniel went inside and grabbed Meryl's car keys. We scraped the ice off the windscreen and set off towards the river. It was an adventure; the roads were completely empty with snow swirling in front of us. We crossed the river at London Bridge, and the Thames spread out on either side. Tower Bridge was all lit up and several of the barges on the river had sprouted Christmas trees. We zoomed along the Embankment, and then we were on Regent's Street under a canopy of Christmas lights. People were everywhere, spilling off the pavement and crossing in front of the car, rushing to get home, heads bowed against the wind and snow, now a mix of colours reflecting the lights above.

'I'd love to have grown up right in the centre of everything,' said Daniel staring at a very rich family emerging from Hamley's Toyshop, laden down with bags.

'I want you in the centre of everything with me,' I said closing my hand over his. We pulled up outside my house just before eight.

'Do you want me to come in with you?' said Daniel.

'No, it's late and... I need to talk to my parents.' My stomach lurched at the thought of going through the front door.

'You don't know how much this means to me, that you've invited us over for Christmas lunch. We get to spend the day together,' he said, his eyes shining excitedly.

'I love you,' I said leaning in for a long deep kiss. 'Sleep tight.' I opened the door and got out. 'Drive safely,' I added.

Daniel grinned and drove away with a wave. I watched the car grow smaller then vanish round the corner. Then I turned and went inside.

I wasn't prepared for the shrill onslaught from Mum when

I came through the front door. She rushed at me in the hallway.

'Where have you been Karen? You left me with hundreds of Turkeys!'

'I was with my boyfriend!' I shouted. 'Okay? I have a boyfriend!'

Dad's eyebrows shot up in surprise.

'What? Who? Who is this boyfriend?' said Mum. 'I hope we know him – and I hope we know him in the right circumstances!'

'You've met him...' I said. 'The Carol singer, Daniel.'

'The one here on the doorstep?'

'Yes.'

Mum clamped her lips together and shook her head.

'You should have seen this boy, Bill, long hair, leather jacket with the hem down, dropped his haitches... Karen, I didn't raise you to go picking up carol singers on the doorstep!'

'Ugh... *Mother*, you are such an ignorant snob!' I shouted.

'Karen,' warned Dad.

'My name is Coco! COCO!!! I met him three months ago, he's at university with me and he's studying music. And I love him!'

'Ok, let's all calm down and let Karen, Coco, come inside,' said Dad. I took off my shoes and followed them through to the living room. My mother sat down in shock.

'Why didn't you tell us?' said Dad.

'Because... You keep going on about Kenneth and how he's perfect for me... and I did want to introduce him to you...but he's not Kenneth. He's better than boring old Kenneth, but *you* don't think that.'

There was silence as they took all this in. The fire crackled.

'Well, maybe we should meet him,' said Dad cautiously, looking over at Mum. She pursed her lips and snorted.

'Well that's handy,' I said, suddenly emboldened with courage. 'Because he's coming over for lunch tomorrow, with his mother and his sister.'

'What?' said Mum leaping off her chair as if someone had shoved a red-hot poker up her bottom.

'I said...'

'I know what you said. You're telling me, after eight o'clock in the evening, that another three people are coming for Christmas lunch, tomorrow!'

'You're already cooking loads of food... And I felt guilty.' I said.

'Why would you feel guilty? Have they got a house? Or are you going to tell me they live in a hut on the Thames?' said Mum.

'They've got a very nice house actually. I feel guilty because it's my fault their turkey ran away.'

'Ran away?' shrieked Mum. 'Why would it run away?'

'Because I left the gate open.'

'You're telling me they keep a turkey in the garden, a real live turkey?'

'Yes.'

'Bill, I think I need a large sherry,' said Mum. Dad jumped up and poured us all one. I could see he was actually quite enjoying this.

'I was cuddling it and I left the gate open and now they haven't got any Christmas lunch,' I repeated.

'Well they should have thought of that before they put themselves in the position of keeping Christmas lunch that could run away... You don't see me keeping pigs in the pantry or a cow in the conservatory.'

'Why do think you're better than everyone else?' I asked.

'I don't think that.'

'Yes, you do.'

'I don't, Karen!'

'Fine, prove me wrong and have them over for lunch.' I said. There was a pause as Dad handed us each a glass of sherry.

'Merry Christmas,' he said.

'Look. I've told them to be here at twelve, so that's when they'll be arriving,' I said downing my sherry in one, and with that, I left the room and went upstairs.

WEDNESDAY 25TH DECEMBER - CHRISTMAS DAY

When I stormed out of the living room last night, I was expecting Mum to follow me upstairs and let me have it, but she didn't. I waited in my room, then I got undressed and lay in bed, but she didn't make an appearance.

This was worrying. She's gone bonkers over far less, like the time I told my friend at school Mum secretly watches Coronation Street with the curtains drawn. She screamed at me about that one for days.

Now, I'd sprung my working class boyfriend and his family on her for Christmas lunch and she was accepting it. Or was she? What did she have planned for me?

When I woke this morning, I quickly got dressed and then poked my head out of my bedroom door. I could smell bacon frying and *Rockin' Around The Christmas Tree* was playing on the radio in the kitchen.

I padded downstairs and, taking a deep breath, went through the swing door into the kitchen. The table was set with a cloth and cutlery and Dad was sitting at the table with a cup of coffee. Mum was artfully arranging bacon and egg on plates.

'Morning,' I said.

'Merry Christmas,' said Mum bringing plates over to the table. She leant in and kissed me on the cheek.

'Merry Christmas, Dad,' I said sitting down, confused.

'Merry Christmas, Coco,' he said with a grin. We started to eat in silence.

'So, this *Daniel chap*,' said Dad. 'Why on earth does he call you Coco?'

'It's silly,' I said.

'It's not some sort of lovey-dovey pet name, is it?' asked Mum trying to hide her revulsion.

'NO!' I said feeling myself go red with horror that they might think I was doing what I actually have done, quite a few times.

'On my first night at Aberystwyth the student's union organised a pub quiz and a raffle, and I won a bottle of Coco Chanel No.5 perfume. Daniel couldn't remember my name so I became the Coco girl, and then everyone started calling me Coco. I like it.'

'So it's a nickname?' said Dad.

'Yes.'

'Well, Happy Christmas, Coco. At least you chose a respectable brand of perfume.'

'That's true. What if it had been Charlie!'

Dad laughed and Mum tried to, which made her look like a snake about to unhinge its jaw.

'Look, Mum, why are you being so calm?' I asked, warily. Mum composed her face into a smile.

'Because I've realised something darling,' she said. 'These people will descend on us for lunch and they'll prove my point that they're not suitable. It won't be nice but I'm willing to go through it all to get this boy out of your system.'

'I'm serious about Daniel,' I said.

'I know you are,' smiled mum patronisingly. 'And despite what you think I won't enjoy seeing you heartbroken.'

Mum seemed so sure of herself, so confident.

'I've already telephoned Yvonne and Adrian, I've warned them what to expect.'

'You've never met Daniel's family!'

'I have a good idea. Now you'll be able to see Daniel and Kenneth side by side and you'll realise just what I see, Kenneth is a catch, and very eligible. I've heard that Yvonne and Adrian are worth well over a million pounds.'

'And that makes them better?'

'Oh darling, you're my daughter and I want the best for you.'

'We both love you,' added Dad.

I realised that this lunch would be a fight, a fight for Daniel and his family, measured against the so-called perfection of the Rosebury's.

'Where are you going?' said Mum as I got up.

'I'm not hungry anymore,' I said. I went and had a shower, and then I shut myself in the airing cupboard with the phone and called Daniel. His mother answered and I heard in the background the sound of him playing *Jingle Bells* on the piano.

''Oo is it?' she shouted.

'It's Coco!'

'Oh 'ello love. John Paul Belmondo is still missin'.'

'I'm so sorry,' I said.

'I went out there this mornin' and made a noise like a girl turkey, but nothin'... 'e's gawn.'

'I'm sorry.' I said again. I tried to imagine Mrs. Pinchard

impersonating a turkey. I had a vision of her pulling her teeth out and crouching down.

'Does yer mum like tinned fruit cocktail?' she asked.

'I think so.'

'Good, 'cos I've got a tin in the cupboard, I won it in the raffle down Hilly Fields. Cost a whole pound for a ticket so it should be good stuff, you know 'ow they sometimes fob you off with peaches and pears an only 'alf a bloomin' cherry!'

'Thank you.'

''Ow about a tin of condensed milk for the pud? An' I think I've got some pickled walnuts in the back of the sideboard...'

'Yes, look can I speak to Daniel please?' I asked, realising that sooner or later Mum would spot the wire for the phone and hoist me out of the cupboard to make brandy butter. The sound of *Jingle Bells* ceased and Daniel was summoned to the phone.

'Merry Christmas, sexy,' he said.

'Look, Daniel,' I said. 'I'm so excited about you all coming, but I have to warn you... there's no other way to say it. My mother is a snob, she looks down on everyone and she's got this awful couple coming called Yvonne and Adrian, with their equally awful son Kenneth who Mum seems to want me to marry. Please just promise you'll still love me afterwards whatever happens?'

'Course I will. You're my Coco. Trust me I can charm the pants off any woman.'

'Daniel!'

'That came out wrong, your pants are the only ones I want to charm off.'

Then I heard his mother shouting, ''Ere Danny 'ave a sniff of these pickled walnuts, are they meant to look like this?'

'Right, I'd better go, see you at twelve,' he said. 'Love you.'
'Love you too,' I said. I wasn't hopeful about lunch.

The Rosebury's rang the doorbell at eleven-thirty. Mum's high heels appeared first as she came running down the stairs. She was wearing the white off-the-shoulder cashmere sweater Dad had given her plus the entire contents of her jewellery box.

'Yvonne!' she cried opening the door where the Rosebury's stood. They stamped the snow off their shoes and came in bearing expensive wine, vintage port, a huge piece of Stilton and a giant bouquet of flowers.

I dreaded what Mum would say when Mrs. Pinchard handed over the condensed milk and tinned fruit.

'Oh! Thank you!' cried Mum. Dad helped Yvonne out of her coat. She was wearing an identical off-the-shoulder cashmere sweater in red.

'You got the Nicole Farhi in cashmere too!' squealed Yvonne as she and Mum admired each other.

'Great minds think alike Bill,' said Adrian gripping my father's hand. Both he and Kenneth were dressed in shirts and ties with dreadful knitted Christmas jumpers.

'Merry Christmas, Bill,' said Adrian pulling out a cigar.

'Merry Christmas, Adrian!' said Dad doing the same. They swapped cigars and held them to their noses.

'This is the life, Bill, rolled on a Cuban virgin's thigh,' said Adrian raising his eyebrows lasciviously. Kenneth stood moodily by the door.

'Karen, say hello to Kenneth and take his coat,' parroted Mum.

'Hello. Coat please,' I said holding out my arm.

49

'Not like you're working in the coat room of a public house... You've got her all flustered Kenneth,' said Mum. Kenneth muttered something neutral.

'I've got my boyfriend coming,' I announced loudly.

'Oh! Boyfriend indeed,' said Adrian, going all bug-eyed at the thought of me being with a boy. 'What does your father think of this?'

'Well, Adrian, he's going to have to come through me first,' said Dad being all comedy macho.

'Oh Kenneth, do give Coco your coat, don't stand on ceremony,' smiled Mum. He handed me his jacket and they all went into the living room. I had to admit, it looked great. The room was candlelit, with fairy lights twinkling on the tree, the fire was burning and holly hung around the mantelpiece. Nat King Cole gently crooned in the background encouraging us all to have a merry little Christmas.

'Oh Evelyn your tree is beautiful,' said Yvonne. Mum did a coquettish little laugh and zipped out, returning with a silver tray with champagne and glasses.

'Bill would you?' asked Mum. Dad started to open the bottle of Moet & Chandon.

'Shampoo eh? Business must be good...' grinned Adrian. Mum subtly twisted the bottle round so the label was showing, and Dad popped the cork. As we clinked glasses Mum started going on about how I'd invited some people over at the last minute, some friends who were having trouble at Christmas. She made it sound like they were coming to us as a soup kitchen!

'It's my boyfriend's family,' I clarified.

'Well, just someone from university,' said Mum airily.

'No. I like Daniel a lot,' I said.

'Well, we'll see about that,' said Mum through gritted teeth.

'You don't get to tell me who I can go out with,' I growled.

'Bill!' shrilled Mum. 'Why don't you take Adrian outside and enjoy those cigars.' The two dads went off gleefully. 'Kenneth, I'm going to show your mother my new Le Creuset range – I got it last week and Delia swears by it. Why don't you talk to Karen about what you're getting up to at Keele.'

Mum ushered Yvonne out leaving Kenneth and me standing awkwardly together.

'So... Is Delia your housekeeper?' asked Kenneth after a pause.

'She means Delia Smith, you know? The television cook?'

'Oh, yeah,' Kenneth nodded, there were droplets of sweat forming on his upper lip.

'Do you want to take that jumper off?' I asked.

'I'm fine,' he snapped.

'Well you don't look it, at least move away from the fire.' He slammed his glass down on the table and yanked his jumper over his head. Underneath he was wearing a starched white shirt and tie.

'Better?' I smiled.

'Yes.'

He folded the jumper up and laid it on the arm of the sofa. We stood in silence.

'Can I just say that I really do have a boyfriend, and despite what our parents want...'

'You can stop flattering yourself,' he said. 'You're hardly my type.'

'What do you mean by that?'

'Well,' he said sneeringly looking me up and down.

'You can piss off!' I snapped. I went to leave but the living room door opened softly and my mother and Yvonne poked their heads inside.

'How are you two getting along?' asked Mum. Yvonne was standing beside her looking equally hopeful.

'Oh *wonderful*,' I said. Kenneth gave me a look.

'Karen! Charge Kenneth's glass,' snapped Mum as if this would make us fall hopelessly in love. They both left the room. I grabbed the glass out of his hand and went to the sideboard. I began pouring more champagne when, through the window into the back garden, I saw a young guy poking his head up over the fence. His hair was gelled up and blow-dried into a Simon Le Bon style, and he had an orange scarf twirled theatrically round his neck. He caught sight of me, stared angrily for a moment then his head vanished.

'God, how long does it take you to pour a drink?' said Kenneth sarcastically.

'There was some guy trying to get over the fence,' I said, handing him his champagne.

'Was it your boyfriend? Trying to escape?' he smirked.

'No this boy was trying to climb in *actually*...'

Kenneth became rather tense.

'Hang on. What did he look like?'

'I dunno. Blond, Simon Le Bon haircut...' Kenneth gulped and gripped his glass harder, and then the doorbell rang. It was Daniel. He was wearing dark trousers and a white shirt open at the neck. His silver St. Christopher glinted against a glimpse of hairy chest. He looked gorgeous.

'Merry Christmas, Coco,' he said leaning in for a kiss.

'Where are your Mum and Meryl?' I asked.

'Oh, um. They're just parking the car,' he grinned.

'There are loads of spaces out the front, aren't there?'

He shrugged oddly and I took him through to the living

room where everyone was now standing with drinks. Mum was a little annoyed at how warmly he was welcomed in. Daniel even called my Dad *Sir,* which earned him several brownie points. Twenty minutes of sipping and chatting passed before Mum started making noises about the dinner being ruined.

'Where did your mum park, Daniel? Tottenham?' I asked. Then the doorbell rang.

'That'll be them,' said Daniel, obviously relieved. Mrs. Pinchard and Meryl were standing on the doorstep with their hair slightly on end as if they'd emerged from a tussle. Meryl smoothed her hair nervously. Mum appeared with Dad, Adrian and Yvonne and they all said an awkward hello.

''Ooh, yer jumper's slipped,' said Mrs. Pinchard pulling Mum's off-the-shoulder firmly back on-the-shoulder. 'Wouldn't want one of yer boobies popping out... well not until we've lit the Christmas pud!'

'It's supposed to be like this,' said Mum, yanking it back down.

'Oh yes,' said Mrs. Pinchard noticing Yvonne. 'The fashion these days!' Dad helped Meryl and Ethel out of their winter coats. Meryl seemed very agitated and barely said hello.

'Oooh, 'ere iss very nice,' said Ethel taking off her headscarf and leaning in to peer up between the bannisters. ''Ave you got the upstairs or the downstairs?'

'The whole house belongs to us!' said Mum, horrified that Ethel might think we only rented – and only part of the house at that. She pulled a face at Yvonne and pulled her into the kitchen. I was left to take everyone into the dining room.

'Did you find a parking space?' I asked.

'What? Oh yeah, yeah...' said Mrs. Pinchard. A look passed between her Meryl and Daniel, but I didn't get a chance to press them further because Mum appeared and banged her little gong.

'Christmas lunch is served,' she said.

'Ooh iss just like them Rank films! You got a man in a loincloth 'oo can do that again!' said Mrs. Pinchard, cackling.

The table was laid out beautifully. I was put between Kenneth and Daniel, and opposite me, Ethel and Meryl were squashed in beside Adrian and Yvonne. Meryl muttered something in Mrs. Pinchard's ear and made as if to get up but Ethel hissed,

'Sit down... Ooh the grub smells lovely!' she added loudly, pulling the ring off her napkin and tucking it into the neck of her blouse. Meryl reluctantly did the same and so did Daniel. Dad came through with the turkey steaming on a huge platter. Yvonne followed with the plates, and Mum rolled in the hostess trolley and began to unload everything onto the table. There was an awesome amount of food. I saw a look shoot between Mum and Yvonne when they saw how my guests were wearing their napkins.

Mrs. Pinchard livened up the proceedings, cutting through the formal atmosphere and encouraging everyone to pull their crackers, put on the silly hats and read out the jokes. My mother was not happy with this. Halfway through another knock knock joke, the front doorbell rang.

'Get that would you, Karen?' said Mum. When I opened the front door the Simon Le Bon guy was standing angrily on the doorstep in his orange scarf.

'Who are you?' he demanded.

'Karen,' I said. 'Who the hell are you?'

'Chris,' said the boy pacing up and down and staring past me into the hallway. 'Is Kenneth in there?'

'Yes. Why do you want to know?'

'I don't know anymore,' he said dramatically. 'I thought I was someone special... Now he's here. With you.'

'What?' I said.

'Oh I'm not going to give you the satisfaction. Go and enjoy your romantic Christmas lunch.'

'What are you talking about?'

'Ask Kenneth!' shrilled Chris and with a flick of his scarf he turned on his heel and marched off down the steps. I closed the door, confused.

'Who was that?' asked Mum when I came back in.

'This really odd chap. He said he knew you, Kenneth, his name's Chris. He was the one peering over the fence earlier.'

Kenneth choked on his sprouts.

'Chris? Chris Cheshire? Blond, about this high?' he asked coughing.

'I suppose so,' I said.

'That's Lord Cheshire's son,' said Yvonne proudly whacking Kenneth on the back. 'Lord Cheshire who owns the napkin empire... He's a friend of Kenneth's. A very good friend. In fact, Kenneth has been to Cheshire Hall no less than three times!'

'Oh Karen, can you see who Kenneth is friends with?' said Mum. She then turned to Daniel's mum who was slurping mashed swede off her desert spoon.

'So, Mrs. Pinchard,' she said baring her teeth and going in for the kill. 'Where do you work?'

'I'm a cleaner, at Catford Police station, and call me Ethel,' she said chewing.

'Oh a *cleaner*,' said Mum. 'Well I suppose someone has to do it.'

'Yeah. It can be a mucky job,' she said oblivious to the sarcasm. 'Do you know, we 'ad a couple of lads in for GBH the night before last, lary as you like. The filthy buggers went on dirty protest! Urgh. You should've seen it... Ooh – that reminds me, Meryl love. You left that yule log in a carrier bag in the hall.'

Meryl jumped up and practically ran out. There was silence, just the sound of knives and forks on china.

''Ere, Adrian, iss come to me now. I knew I recognised you,' said Mrs. Pinchard fixing her gaze on him.

'Ooh, I love a mystery,' he grinned.

'Actual Bodily Harm weren't it? You were mixed up in that Millwall business last month. I cleaned out the cell they put you in.'

Adrian's face dropped.

'What? Oh, no that wasn't me.'

'Yes! You and yer mate got arrested for peeing in a post box after the match. Then you slapped that copper round the chops.'

Mum and Dad looked at Adrian in dismay.

'It must be someone else, Mrs. Pinchard, you sound like you don't come north of the river often,' said Mum nervously.

'No 'e came south, I never forget a face,' said Mrs. Pinchard pointing at Adrian with a roasted parsnip.

'Well, ha ha, it was just a silly thing that got out of hand at a football match,' said Adrian.

'You smacked a copper in the gob, that 'aint just silly. When's your court date?' said Mrs. Pinchard.

We all froze at the table.

'OOOH! You're such a thug!' screamed Yvonne suddenly out of character. 'I knew people would find out! You're strutting around the place like Lord Muck with your bloody cigars!' She threw her napkin down and left the room in tears. Adrian jumped up.

'Thank you very much!' hissed Adrian and followed Yvonne.

'What? I'm not the one 'oo did in that copper,' said Mrs. Pinchard to the horrified table. 'Nice lad 'e is too...'

At that moment we heard a scream from Yvonne.

'Oh Bill, do you think Adrian's attacking Yvonne?' asked Mum in horror. We all jumped up and rushed into the hall. The front door was open and, bizarrely, Meryl was staggering in under the weight of John Paul Belmondo, the Christmas turkey. His huge wings were flapping as she tried to keep hold of him. Yvonne was screaming in terror.

'What the bloody 'ell are you doin' Meryl!' shouted Mrs. Pinchard.

'He was scratching the upholstery of my car!' she said apologetically. 'Will someone help me carry him through to the back garden!'

'What in God's name?' said Mum.

'We found 'im 'alfway up the Old Kent Road, I couldn't leave 'im! I thought 'e'd be alright in the car while we 'ad lunch!' said Mrs. Pinchard. 'It were Coco 'oo lost 'im in the first place!' she added.

Meryl lost her grip on John Paul and he jumped out of her arms and into the hall. Yvonne screamed in terror and Adrian kicked out at him. John Paul quite rightly got upset and started to hiss and spit with his wings flapping. They scarpered into the dining room, the angry turkey half running half flying after them.

We followed and found Yvonne and Adrian standing at the far end of the dining table. John Paul Belmondo was on the table with his impressive wingspan fully deployed, beak down and advancing towards them knocking over glasses. Yvonne's lipsticked mouth was stretched wide in horror and then John

Paul charged forward and they all disappeared under the table.

'I won't take this!' shouted a voice. We turned to find Chris, the Simon Le Bon guy standing in the dining room doorway. He must have come in through the open front door.

'I love you Kenneth Rosebury,' he shrilled. 'I deserve to eat Christmas lunch with you. I refuse to be a dirty secret! Let's stop creeping around. Let's be out and proud!'

No-one took much notice as there were terrible sounds coming from under the dining table.

'My mother's being attacked by an eagle!' shouted Kenneth.

'It's a bloody turkey you prat!' shouted Mrs. Pinchard as Chris dived under the table and managed to wrangle John Paul just enough so that Yvonne and Adrian could escape.

An hour later I was standing on the doorstep with Daniel and Chris. Meryl and Ethel had managed to sedate John Paul with a teaspoon of cooking sherry and get him back into the car.

He was sitting apologetically on the back seat, his eyes sad once more. I said goodbye to Meryl and she got in the driver's side.

'We'll take 'im back 'ome, get 'im settled in the yard. Thanks for lunch love,' said Mrs. Pinchard. 'Ooh I forgot to give these to your mum, she'll think I've got no manners!' She handed me some tinned fruit and pickled walnuts. I was lost for words as she waved goodbye and they drove off with John Paul Belmondo's head poking out of the back window.

Mum and Dad had taken Yvonne and Adrian to the casualty department at Guy's and St. Thomas's Hospital. I think it was mostly for shock. They emerged fairly unscathed and the only thing that would require stitches was Yvonne's Nicole Farhi cashmere sweater.

As we walked up to the front door Kenneth was leaving.

'Stay away from me,' he shouted and ran past us without a word of goodbye. Chris was in tears so I asked him to stay for a bit.

'I'm sorry I barged in and ruined your Christmas day,' said Chris as we all sat by the fire with the rest of the champagne.

'I think it had already gone down the pan when the turkey went on the rampage,' I grinned.

'And when my mum outed your friend's father as a police beater,' added Daniel.

'And then you outed their son as... well you outed him. It was far more interesting than our normal Christmas,' I said, and we all burst out laughing.

'I don't know if he'll ever speak to me again,' said Chris. 'I love him.'

'You could do so much better than Kenneth Rosebury,' I said. 'Anyway, he's up at university in Keele, I take it you live in London?'

'Yeah. My parents just bought me a cottage by Regent's Park... Where I'm going to die alone!' he added mournfully.

'Well I'm here,' I said kindly. 'And you really impressed me with how you wrestled with John Paul Belmondo.'

'Really?' he said, wiping the tears off his face.

'Yeah, your hair didn't move.'

'Aquanet hairspray. I swear by it. Look, here's my phone number,' he said handing me a card. 'I hope you'll ring me, Coco.'

Chris left when the champagne ran out. He invited us to a club in the West End but we promised we'd do it some other time. It had started to snow again when we came back inside. I surveyed the mess in the dining room. I went to pick up a broken plate but Daniel put his hand over mine.

'They'll be gone hours at the hospital.'

'Yes they will,' I said. 'Here, I haven't had my Christmas present from you yet.'

We went and sat by the fire again and swapped gifts. I'd bought him the new Kate Bush record *Hounds of Love* which he was thrilled with. He then handed me a little box. I opened it and nestled inside was a silver chain.

'Oh Daniel, it's beautiful,' I cried. He lifted up my hair and gently fastened it around my neck.

'I want to be with you always Coco,' he said. 'And every year we're together I want to buy you a beautiful piece of jewellery.'

Well that was it. If I wasn't hopelessly in love with him before, I was now. We cuddled up together by the fire as the dusk fell and snow drifted softly past the window.

'Will you marry me Coco?' he whispered quietly in my ear. I closed my eyes, lay my head against his chest and felt his strong heart beating.

'Yes, Daniel,' I said. 'Yes, I'll marry you...'

A NOTE FROM ROBERT

Hello, and a huge thank you for choosing to read *A Very Coco Christmas*. If you did enjoy it, I would be very grateful if you could tell your friends and family. Word-of-mouth is one of the most effective ways of recommending a book, and it helps me reach out and find new readers. Your endorsement makes a big difference! You could also write a product review. It needn't be long, just a few words, but this also helps new readers find one of my books for the first time.

I've written in the back of the previous Coco Pinchard novels that I would love to hear from you, and you've done me proud. Thank you for all your messages!

If you want to get in touch, you can find me via my website www.robertbryndza.com

If you enjoyed *A Very Coco Christmas* you should check out my second Coco Pinchard Christmas novella, *Coco Pinchard's Must-Have Toy Story*, where Coco has to track down the must-have Christmas toy for four-year-old Rosencrantz!

Robert Bryndza

ABOUT THE AUTHOR

Robert Bryndza is an international bestselling author, best known for his page-turning crime and thriller novels, which have sold over four million copies in the English language.

His crime debut, *The Girl in the Ice* was released in February 2016, introducing Detective Chief Inspector Erika Foster. Within five months it sold one million copies, reaching number one in the Amazon UK, USA and Australian charts. To date, *The Girl in the Ice* has sold over 1.5 million copies in the English language and has been sold into translation in 29 countries. It was nominated for the Goodreads Choice Award for Mystery & Thriller (2016), the Grand prix des lectrices de Elle in France (2018), and it won two reader voted awards, The Thrillzone Awards best debut thriller in The Netherlands (2018) and The Dead Good Papercut Award for best page turner at the Harrogate Crime Festival (2016).

Robert has released a further five novels in the Erika Foster series, *The Night Stalker, Dark Water, Last Breath, Cold Blood* and *Deadly Secrets*, all of which have been global bestsellers, and in 2017 *Last Breath* was a Goodreads Choice Award nominee for Mystery and Thriller.

Most recently, Robert created a new crime thriller series based around the central character Kate Marshall, a police officer turned private detective. The first book, *Nine Elms*, was an Amazon USA #1 bestseller and an Amazon UK top five bestseller, and the series has been sold into translation in 15 countries. The second book, *Shadow Sands* was an Amazon charts and Wall Street Journal bestseller, and the third book, *Darkness Falls* will be published shortly.

Robert was born in Lowestoft, on the east coast of England. He studied at Aberystwyth University, and the Guildford School of Acting, and was an actor for several years, but didn't find success until he took a play he'd written to the Edinburgh Festival. This led to the decision to change career and start writing. He self-published a bestselling series of romantic comedy novels, before switching to writing crime. Robert lives with his husband in Slovakia, and is lucky enough to write full-time.

Printed in Great Britain
by Amazon